The
Last
Usable
Hour

The Last Usable Hour

DEBORAH LANDAU

COPPER CANYON PRESS

PORT TOWNSEND, WASHINGTON

Printed in the United States of America

Cover Art: Matthea Harvey, *One Chair,* 2007. Digital photograph.

Copper Canyon Press is in residence at Fort Worden State Park
in Port Townsend, Washington, under the auspices of Centrum.
Centrum is a gathering place for artists and creative thinkers
from around the world, students of all ages and backgrounds, and
audiences seeking extraordinary cultural enrichment.

LIBRARY OF CONGRESS CATALOGING-IN-PUBLICATION DATA

Landau, Deborah
The last usable hour / Deborah Landau.
    p. cm.
ISBN 978-1-55659-334-5 (pbk.)
I. Title.
PS3612.A54755L37 2011
811'.6—dc22

                             2011001332

98765432 First Printing

Copper Canyon Press
Post Office Box 271
Port Townsend, Washington 98368
www.coppercanyonpress.org

Grateful acknowledgment is made to the editors of the following publications in which versions of these poems originally appeared: *Alaska Quarterly Review, The Awl, The Cincinnati Review, Harvard Review, The Kenyon Review, Maggy, Michigan Quarterly Review, The Paris Review, Subtropics, Tin House, TriQuarterly,* and *Washington Square.*

Poems were reprinted in *Alhambra Poetry Calendar 2009* and *2011, Disco Prairie Social Aid and Pleasure Club,* and *Poetry Daily.*

I would like to thank the generous friends who offered helpful suggestions on earlier drafts of this manuscript. Special thanks to Catherine Barnett, Meghan O'Rourke, and Matthew Zapruder, for their literary companionship and close attention to these poems. Much gratitude also to Michael Wiegers and everyone at Copper Canyon Press.

for Mark

Contents

The
Last
Usable
Hour

I

All Else Fails

*

I'd rather watch you doing it
than do it myself.
I'd rather hear about it.
I want to be told.
I'd rather read about it.
I'd rather just sit here.
Hold the mask over my face
while you do it to me.
I'll put on some music.
Now see how we grow aglow
so young and beautiful
our capillaries all lit up.

*

Days, weeks, months
why not use them for something?
I'm heading for a head-on.
I'm revving up my so-called self.
I know my life is meaning
less. Strutting around
for a while until poof.

Everything gets more and more absurd.
The office and deskchair, the skin on the neck
eye cream, love, the hand-holding and bungled
attempts, watching the clock all night—2 a.m., 4
then daylight, sitting in my dress again
with cup and plate.
To work to work then back again
to bed, another night.

*

I read Pessoa and he confirms
my worst suspicions.

I read the entertaining novels
and they make me happy.

I sleep beside the river.
The river often sleeps when I'm awake.

Sky, water, I have not had enough of you.
Better be shoving off again and into the night.

*

More and more it's deliciousness I want
but all the time there's less of it.
What the hell do you think you're doing?
You should find something definite to subscribe to
so as not to keep drifting tossed aimless through the world like this.
At the party Stanley said for now factor in gratitude
narrow the zone and see your life
which is what we call it as if it were a real thing.
I wear my street clothes. I accept the parameters.
Don't shout drink some wine at night
work is what is offered and sometimes love.
Another time there was ecstasy
though many things went laughably wrong.

*

Those who don't feel
are happy
says Pessoa.

Those who don't think.

The night has advanced.
We figure in it so slightly.

Down the ice chute we go.

Say goodbye to your eyes in real time.
Get ready, get set. Say goodbye

to your synovial fluid. Your knees
will wear out in no time

won't hoist you nowhere.

*

In the middle of my wood, I found myself in a dark life.
The day was going toward the narrow place the blank.
No matter how many glasses of gin
it will get dark on this platform of earth.
When with your milk and fruit
when with your wine
when with your mirror and your little book
you sit tableside in the candlelit clearing
when with your warm breath
are you sick
are you all done flirting
have you lost your appetites
no longer a girl but slinking around nonetheless.

*

He keeps me waiting
and I start hysteria a little bit.
I start hysteria against everyone's advice.
I go into the street to drink air.
I've never been so thirsty in my life.
Another mouth, some fresh-minted lips.
See, I can feel blue on half a bottle of jewels.
Sleep then wake then this then that day
and another night back on the bed
lying in an eros dumb and slackjawed.
The sound of hustling advances and retreats
as if someone were shuffling money
or unbuttoning a blouse.
Can you put that taffeta away now, please?
Please put it away.

＊

As soon as he sits down I can tell I want to.
How long can I sit here not doing the thing
I want to do. All the youngish men
all the etceteras of desire, etcetera.
There's a little hole in my boot.
Could you put your finger in it?
There is power in breathing.
There is power in a silent beat
before answering a question, in a leaning in.
Across the table his mind right there
behind his talking face.

*

We're in a dirty place now
when we get together.
We made a nasty city
and have to live in it.
Before we were wider wilder avenues
but we made it too
cramped and ugly.
Nowhere to go to tea.
Only gin here
and no god at any gate
and no goodness.

*

Now our bed is not ample not fair. Now
we don't have a bed
only this corner blackred and backlit.
Something of me is a blind point, something of him, too.
There's a little edge of pain here and we walk along it.
Don't cry, don't kiss me either, and also don't stop.
That's the way he looks when he wants to watch.
Why don't you go swoon yourself into some fantastic
mood music. I am a small cup with a twist
and you are liquid. A drink.
Another drink.

An emptiness of shoes, enough to overdose on
some faded solitudes, fields
wardrobes of dead people, wideleaved froth
cool liquor, its quiet swirl in Andrew's glass
my desire to drink from it.
Remember the cleft of summer
how lithe it all looked, how august.
December is the season of which
the many facets and flats are made.
The flood of the dull with its million holes
interwoven with the honeysweet.
The return of the approaching year.
Now see what can be made into a narcotic goblet
what can be made of dusk, its many openings.

II

Blue Dark

*

if the soul
sits outside the body

if the body
stays put
in its slated bed

if there is a blue
arm of sleep

if there is a waking
and an appetite

and it's morning
and the blood
will still pulse

*

I'm thinking of
you tonight Philip
Larkin groping back
to bed after
a piss
and yes
the moon
so cold
through the bars
on the window
the empty
southward
sky
(there's so much
of it now)
and here
in my
narrow bed

*

the night has no cracks
nothing haunts the highways
the president speaks
from the big lit screens
but he speaks to no one
all night the hudson river
runs blank and gray
beneath the window
for someone else to see
no one left in the city
no one in the fields
no one coming no one going
I'm alone
with the small discomforts
that drift me from bed
to the television
where no one is left
but the president
on every channel
water falling over brick
water over bone
over maiden lane
and the new york sports club
and the south street seaport
and wendy's on water street
it's reached the end
at the end of the room
and left a sick print on the carpet

*

and so the evening wears on
urging me to remove my petticoats

little batch of twitchings

while outside another balcony
fills with

the wind against the other panes
blowing hard all night

city of spirit city of soil
back alley and dumpster
& stiff-pricked whomever—

outside rain is soaking the alleys
rarer and wilder

*

well now
underneath the whispering
underneath the darkness
listen hard
gunmetal end of winter
too cold to undress
underneath the whispering
underneath the darkness

*

and I couldn't bear it
the children nearing the place
where the waves wet the shore

vaporous force
rising imperceptibly behind

we were talking about circumstance
horizon-gates swinging open
beneath the cherry blooms

wave rising in the background
impalpable and final
a girl in a white dress   barefoot

wasn't I right to ask her to move in from the shore

*

since only the physical exists
we stood in the cemetery
and worked from above

the trees shot straight up
in translation

the children went celebrating
the presence of stones

I saw on every side
men women mothers
lifted and missing

the mothers gone down cold
in the sweater of dirt

I looked and saw my body
not near yours but far
not lying beside but away

two bodies in the fields
the sky frigid starred

our callow tagged still-aliveness
the sinking tide of voices
and flowering gallow-cloth

the lull mothers coming and going
the lulling gone and gentler

one by one
until the world is peopled
with ghosts

once most vivid alive

*

dark upholstered by snow
will you accumulate?

I dreamed your myriad deaths
went erased

and the pencil disappeared
into paper

and night lightened
from the top down

and between here and there
the hallway

at the end of which
you stand

dark light streams

flutter passes through it
iridescent and not lovely

*

& certain places on earth
evoke this blank shining

a beaded necklace   red wine
someone's voice sings

this single loneliness yellows
goes on breathing
all night

as if it were natural

*

the trouble with silence
is the high square room
hymnless and the window
opening on a blank
the trouble with silence is creation
farewell the glistening mouth
the trouble with silence
oh mother
the trouble
the harmless pleasures
and the ones that come to harm
in the fields
in the central city
the trouble with silence
is none ever was

*

siren-wracked
river-bordered
pigeon-shitted
skyline bunched
and branchless

the sleepers stacked
and caged

the thousand thousand souls
opening and closing
at will in the stillness

the country at work
in deft
and viperous ways

and we are in it
hard and breakable

new york
city of hidden interiors

the old black streets
and the old night sky

and passing by
of one
or of another one
who is dead and wants
to see me

*

far from here in the burial grounds
each fits neatly next to the other

see how the dirt grows around us
why don't you come to bed

a living room of quiet

such spooked radiance
the creeping up of it

goodbye to the rabbi
goodbye to the mourners

the bibles   the body
held up to the light

we left the dead in the fields
the bread on the table

we left the dead in the fields
we left them reclining

away from the fields we had matted down
away from the grass worn in places the grass matted

and brown   away from the sun on the wood
as the wood was lowered

we left the dead in the fields
we left the book on the traytable

washed our hands
as the train moved through

the bright Boston-bound afternoon
we left the dead in the fields

we were heading for the sloughing off
we were on the banks of it

III

Someone

*

forgive me for not sleeping
this city is all spinning   all sky

this city is dry and the people all wanting
each with a coin purse   each with a thirst in her mouth

dear someone   I put a shimmer on for you
tonight I am all sequins   all lies

for you I've slit my skirt
made a neckhole of longing

I am always nighttime on the inside
barefoot and heretic

I need god or at least the police

say there are no more empty places
say you will sleep again in my bed

lie down

let the night pour up through us
fluid cherry dark

others are lying down

bedrooms are going red with it
all over this town

*

dear someone

I was ruminating
in a January of park

mild and bare-branched

gray entourage
of buildings

and the skyline
how I like it

pressing up
against my neck

your hand
felt cool to the touch

my skirt swept upward
a substitute for speaking

*

then we were actual people
your actual mouth on mine

my hangup
on your answering machine

now you are here
and never here

now you go by
as I turn in my sleep

now it's the spring
of the sick birds

of the too hot
too soon unoriginal

magnolia
explosions

spring of the jewel-green
parakeet

open-beaked
on the pavement

spring of your great
big empty emotionless face

*

dear someone

see how you have entered my house
and so lightly remain

3 a.m.   the blue dark
snow on the fire escape

the smell of diesel   your hand
on my soft places   trucks shattering

broome street   your hand
up my nightgown   I wish

you wouldn't do that   bang
of the radiator   sirens

on Broadway
your snowmelter fingers

I wish you would

the view is river
the view is black
and a little beyond

and you
you is heavy
you is a slow tune

rough penciled
wool and silk sack
and the face of snow

how you come
and undo my clasp

*

dear someone
so strange to see you today

taking up more than your share
of space

we meet at the café
because you are waiting there

dear someone
where did you buy your scarf

do you like it
I do

*

immaculate middle-of-the-night quiet

rainlessness

the late moony sadness
of the one specific mosquito

dear someone

you habituate me to the invisible
I exit through you not as myself

*

dear someone
let's screw and make it final
then recline and be complete

in evening   in nether
in darkscarlet sinking
a gigantic slowing down

there!   I have put my lips on
done good and well the sacred sealing

here's a cure for sullen   for spring
for love   for love's absence

let's measure up in the vestibule
knee deep in it   mud-weedy
and uncovered   uncovered all over

*

more is more

which is why
we perverse ourselves

into the many shapes we make
spared the separation

praise
the with-joy

your lower
between my

conjoined
open-necked
smutting in
and out of it

happy
have us all inside

*

blame the egg   blame the fractured stones
at the bottom of the mind

blame his darkblue glare and craggy mug
the bulky king of trudge and stein

how I love a masculine in my parlor
his grizzly shout and weight   one hundred drums

in this everywhere of blunt and soft sinking
I am the heavy hollow   snared

the days are spring   the days are summer
the days are nothing and not dead yet

*

dear someone

your emptiness has a lake in it   deep and watery
with several temperaments   milk cola beer

at night the selves are made of water
all the openings flooded   streaming with rain

your emptiness has an aqueduct in it
selves rushing through channels

dissolving   washing away in streaks

your emptiness has a fish in it
a piece of seaweed   liferaft   a rocky strait

all night the selves are breaking themselves
again and again on the sandbar

you can't get out from the drowning
nightwatery   the blacksparkling pools

your emptiness has a nowhere reef   an island
at night the immersion comes deep-running and sudden

the selves
it washes us under and sudden

*

all night the moon insists on being right
and central   its nothing glare limning the pane

shutters stuck flush to the sides of the building
some sorry streetlamp spreading its cold

dear someone
what happened to the story the dream the you
bending over roses in back of the house

bring back your onset   your velvet
and I'll apply it

my gorgeous   my immaculate
my favorite dirty most unrequited

we'll be dark-hinged and planetary
drifting in and out of every season

*

dear someone
I have nearly completed
your disappearance

I spent all night
collecting your photographs
and cutting them up

a little black hair
a little lip and finger

close your eyes
only your little time here and you breathing

no steps in the hallway
only your horizontal bones laid out on the bed

look   it is early winter
the doors are open

you are floating alone
in the cold blue

these are the hours of blankness

all the walls are bare

*

sometimes there would be story
the end the last line
and someone reading it
word by word in the dark
dear someone
we were a happy medley
we were under a roof
we were at rest and breathing
away from lovely death
retold and told
until it reaches the rest point
until the wavering stops
and the mirror that shows
your strange face
returns you still here
dear someone
thanks for the dream
you leave a deep blue crease
in the center of my day
dear someone
it was all in error
no way to get back
no records left
but empty now
and blued like a room
the projector's gone off
mostly dreams reject us
lights go up at daybreak
no reentry

IV

Welcome to the Future

*

so it came time and
no day like that is ever
good in the coming
the satin bleeding
the river flowing down
and heavy and to the east
dark with soot
crossing the night bridge
the river flowing down
and heavy and to the east
there were roads into bitter
heads between knees
the diminishing systems
bleached and diagonal
the river flowing down
down and no sound

*

welcome to the future

I have come into the aware
where the gilt edges are

look all the men
and the distance sitting in the roar
with darkened blue glass

we are aware
as if all is tunnel and paper

there are bodies and
bills in these flattened villas

one waves as I pass him

and home isn't here
and home isn't there

and randomly we plead with the officers
to get down from their cophorses and help us

*

Richard propped up the bottles
like bowling pins

I had fallen into despair
did this bother him

when Richard left I broke
my throat I bit my tongue

cracked teeth my mouth split my lip
smashed chairs in the bar trashed

poems I was writing
all this breaking was very expensive

there is no Richard but I think it was Richard
who had the idea of pouring libations

because of the stumbling thirst
because our lives are like that

I am writing this to do as right as possible by Richard
think back to the bed consider the bar

the fragrant medicinal flasks
I don't care to drink anymore because when I drink

it makes me hopeless
Richard, are you going to come back

to the bar where you belong
or just leave me here

here is a flask
I am tired of being metaphysical

our bar is a winter bar
at night we need the dream

of all the objects lined up in a row

*

sometimes he writes his name inside here
sometimes he scratches it in
sometimes he wields the invisible sticks
steadily and with even hand
with the syringe he takes me down the hill
and along the wall to the empty field
to cease the small animals
to cease the car driving down the road
the bird dipping into the orchard
by the time we get to the river
he's ballistic   trying to remember
the names of trees
the way to the nearest park
he keeps at it   pacing the invisible evening
all night I lie on the forest floor
all night is long enough

*

worry the river over its banks
the train into flames

worry the black rain into the city
the troops into times square

worry the windows cracked acidblack
and the children feverblistered

worry never another summer
never again to live here gentle
with the other inhabitants

then leave too quickly
leave the pills and band-aids
the bathroom scale the christmas lights the dog

go walking on our legs
dense and bare and useless

worry our throats and lungs
into taking the air

leave books on the shelves
leave keys   dustpan

telephones don't work   where you were
in the chaos

*

desolate oblivion face me along the bar
nothing will rest tonight in the high empty room

the nothing closes forever
in a shopwindow
and forever opens the heads wide again

height is felled   wire rises
the glass is laced together with tunnels

the fathers are all glass
all air and windows

*

the train
came racing
into the station
the shining
seats
the vacant
cars
and I
the only
I
and death
in the air
like the smell
of tunnels
beautiful
and defaced

*

tonight the backyard is brutal
in its twilit emptiness
& I have put my lips
on the glass of his face again
so I won't be lonely
& I have dressed to please him
because it's too quiet here
my hand alive in the cage of his
an actual dandelion in the grass
beside his sandal
the mosquitoes grazing our ankles
we should go inside he says
as the pitchblack comes on again like arsenic
over the glowing lawn

*

to stay here
would be
contentment
would be
an afterlife
exaltation
would be
unmatchably
satisfying
but darling
happiness
is provincial
yet just now
we are here
and want
nothing
maybe melancholy
is overrated
leave it
behind
awhile

*

with his words
in my head
I slept for thirty
or forty forevers
while the grass shrieked
and the trees tremored
it was crazy
letting my youth
pass like that
giving myself up
to the abstract fears
balconies collapsing
over the east river
as far as the eye could see
until all is miniature
wind over water
without end
when I am dead
I will have something
to say about death
& all the men stretched out
a girl must be a graveyard
I am a descendant of fields
and want to keep my mind off it, especially

*

gadgets can save you from shatter
mustard jars can be clean
can be stacked in a row
I fill the tubs with rainwater
I fill the buckets I flood the sinks
it comforts me to do it
empty bottles have a perfect shelflife
empty bottles make a perfect afterlife
I have saved all my dimes
I breathe in time with the ticking
I make the same movements
repeat the same words I hear on tv
from all these corks
I am building a boat
that will take me out of this city
that will take me all the way

bombing in the dark makes a mess for later
shatter can be stored in a vial in a jar
shards can be icy can be in between tables
and stuck in the palpable cord
they found the dog he was facing down
you can feed him
but he will never again be even a little bit alive

the bombs will fall in the garden the bombs will fall in the jail
at first they'll sound like rain
then they'll sound a different spectrum
the bombs have to glass through the restaurant
until the splintered minutes are up
dinner is over and the world is wrong
certain questions hang in the mind
you can't tell where the limbs are exactly

*

subway reeks river reeks
hot city reeks in the dawn
the world gives up its divine
and pleasing odors
even the little girls reek
in their lace-trimmed socks
and the bankers and thicknecked
criminals locked in their cells
and we are in it
hard and mineral
moving into the headwound
with our edges rolled back

*

then the cave of humanfruit turns liquid
a steel sharps the everything
of walls and wineglasses
and splits the screen with red effort
apocalypse televised
the explosions increase
a sun here
and there split asunder
and shake out blades
rocking a faint moan
as they beat
against the white something
chairs tables tablecloths falling
muffled on the wires
the edges breaking

*

the water runs shallow
and midnight presents
the dried-up riverbed
moonless and rocky
night's dark and empty bottom
where mrs. prone
lies stranded
without her stockings
without her shoes
I don't sleep
why should I
it would only debase
my dreambody
all night the linens breathe
in a silent way
lit by echoingmind
I try to sleep
I come to silence
in one of the hells
run back into it
then down the same abyss
I don't see when I wake
any happiness
the scent is undressing
the scent is an old field
whose gate had seemed to be part of me

*

this is the last usable hour

bird lured
through the window

a little sweet fruit

I could die here
and the hearsedriver
would take me out of this city

I'd say my name to him
as we crossed the Triboro

I'd say it softly   the way he likes it

it would be the last time
I'd introduce myself that way

About the Author

Deborah Landau is the author of one previous book of poetry, *Orchidelirium*. Her poems have appeared in numerous magazines and anthologies including *The Kenyon Review, The Paris Review, Tin House,* and *The Best American Erotic Poems.* She lives in New York City, where she directs the Creative Writing Program at New York University.

Since 1972, Copper Canyon Press has fostered the work of emerging, established, and world-renowned poets for an expanding audience. The Press thrives with the generous patronage of readers, writers, booksellers, librarians, teachers, students, and funders — everyone who shares the belief that poetry is vital to language and living.

Copper Canyon Press gratefully acknowledges board member

JIM WICKWIRE

for his many years of service to poetry and independent publishing.

Major support has been provided by:

Amazon.com

Anonymous

Beroz Ferrell & The Point, LLC

Golden Lasso, LLC

Gull Industries, Inc.
on behalf of William and Ruth True

Lannan Foundation

Rhoady and Jeanne Marie Lee

National Endowment for the Arts

Cynthia Lovelace Sears and Frank Buxton

Washington State Arts Commission

Charles and Barbara Wright

*To learn more about underwriting
Copper Canyon Press titles, please call
360-385-4925 x103*

Lannan Literary Selections

For two decades Lannan Foundation has supported the
publication and distribution of exceptional literary works.
Copper Canyon Press gratefully acknowledges their support.

LANNAN LITERARY SELECTIONS 2011

Michael Dickman, *Flies*

Laura Kasischke, *Space, in Chains*

Deborah Landau, *The Last Usable Hour*

Valzhyna Mort, *Collected Body*

Dean Young, *Fall Higher*

RECENT LANNAN LITERARY SELECTIONS
FROM COPPER CANYON PRESS

Stephen Dobyns, *Winter's Journey*

David Huerta, *Before Saying Any of the Great Words: Selected Poems,*
translated by Mark Schafer

Sarah Lindsay, *Twigs and Knucklebones*

Heather McHugh, *Upgraded to Serious*

W.S. Merwin, *Migration: New & Selected Poems*

Taha Muhammad Ali, *So What: New & Selected Poems, 1971–2005,*
translated by Peter Cole, Yahya Hijazi, and Gabriel Levin

Travis Nichols, *See Me Improving*

Lucia Perillo, *Inseminating the Elephant*

James Richardson, *By the Numbers*

Ruth Stone, *In the Next Galaxy*

John Taggart, *Is Music: Selected Poems*

Jean Valentine, *Break the Glass*

C.D. Wright, *One Big Self: An Investigation*

For a complete list of Lannan Literary Selections from
Copper Canyon Press, please visit Partners on our Web site:
www.coppercanyonpress.org

The poems are set in Minion. The headings are set in Letter Gothic. Book design and composition by Phil Kovacevich. Printed on archival-quality paper at McNaughton & Gunn, Inc.

The Chinese character for poetry is made up of two parts: "word" and "temple." It also serves as pressmark for Copper Canyon Press.